To Dustin,
Good things happen
when you work hard!

Scott Woerner

GAME DAY
GEORGIA FOOTBALL

GAME DAY
GEORGIA FOOTBALL

*The Greatest Games, Players, Coaches and Teams
in the Glorious Tradition of Bulldog Football*

**TRIUMPH
BOOKS**
CHICAGO

Athlon® Sports™
AMERICA'S PREMIER SPORTS ANNUALS

Library of Congress Control Number: 2005905674

This book is available in quantity at special discounts for your group or organization.
For further information, contact:

Triumph Books
542 South Dearborn Street
Suite 750
Chicago, Illinois 60605
(312) 939-3330
Fax (312) 663-3557

EDITORS: Rob Doster, Kevin Daniels

PHOTO EDITOR: Tim Clark

DESIGN: Anderson Thomas Design

PHOTO CREDITS:
Georgia Sports Information: Pgs. 10, 26, 30-49, 51, 60-63, 76-83, 86-91, 94-98, 121, 122, 125-129, 131, 140-147; Getty Images: Pg. 74 Jamie Squire, Pg. 99 Erik Lesser; Clate Sanders pg 111; Randy Miller pg 109; Wingate Downs pgs. 109, 106, 107; All others from Athlon Archive

Printed in U.S.A

ISBN-13: 978-1-57243-761-6
ISBN-10: 1-57243-761-8

CONTENTS

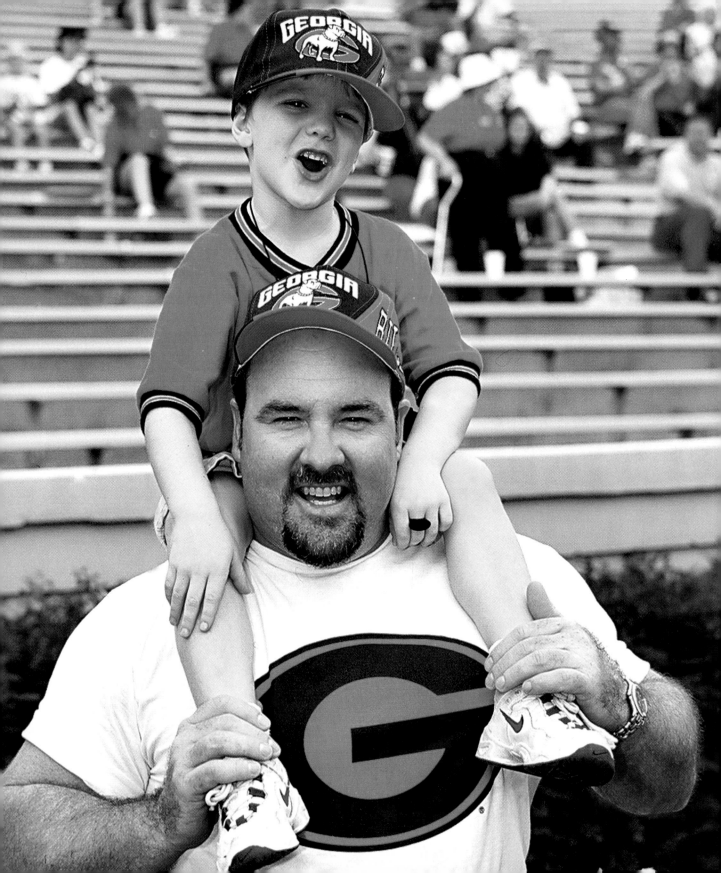

Foreword

So, how do you introduce a book on the history of Georgia football? Oddly enough, I'll start in Colorado.

In the fall of 1945, I was broadcasting my first home game with the Second Air Force football team from Colorado Springs. It was a typical service football game between two powerhouse teams that were both filled up with All-American football players who had spent their war years playing an exceptionally high brand of college football. In the very first quarter of that game, they carried a Second Air Force running back off the field on a stretcher. His name was Frank Sinkwich.

It was a bad moment for Sinkwich because the knee injury kept him from a pro football career. But at that time, I wasn't familiar with him and had no idea that many years later I would be working the broadcasts for Georgia, where Sinkwich had made quite a name for himself before enlisting in the Air Force.

We really shouldn't even mention Georgia football without going back into the memory banks and finding all the names that meant so much to you and me both. From Trippi to Rauch, Butts, Tarkenton, Sapp, McClendon, Arnold, Butler, Bennett, Herschel, Zeier, Etter, Moore, Patton, Stanfill, Lawrence,

Greene, Pollack, Dooley, etc. . . . See how easy it is to start writing about Georgia football when you find yourself covered up with hundreds of names from the past? Some of them from the very recent past?

I grew up in a Big Ten house; everybody followed the University of Minnesota, and everybody always cursed the University of Michigan. They also threw a few words out there against Iowa, Wisconsin, Notre Dame and Purdue. Never did I dream that I would wind up in the South directing my hatred against General Bob Neyland, Steve Spurrier, Pat Dye and Danny Ford—not to mention any jersey that was covered with orange. As my 40 years of working Georgia football unfolded, many of the Big Ten teams were starting to decline, while the SEC was flying high and continues to climb even higher.

I've had 56 years in the SEC now, and I have no way of knowing all the great teams and where they should be ranked. But I do know this: Georgia football fans are as rabid and passionate as they come. I've been here so long now, I can't even remember when tailgating started! That goes back to the '60s. I think, however, the food now is much better, and there is much more of it.

We've turned the century mark now, and with it all the stadiums have grown twice as big, and the press boxes are also spread out all over the place. Unfortunately, the radio booths are now seven miles from the field. At least, it seems that way.

And now, here comes my 40th year of working Georgia football; the old names and games should be distant memories, but they continue to leap to my mind. With all the major names that left us a few months ago, how are we going to remember the 2004 team, I wonder? I also can't help but wonder if Buck and Lindsay and a fullback named Haynes are also overwhelmed by the great memories flooding their memory banks.

As we look forward to making more memories together, I have a thought: wouldn't it be great to play Southern Cal in the Rose Bowl? Would we all walk away satisfied then?

—LARRY MUNSON

Introduction

Georgia football has a language all its own. "Hunker down, you hairy Dawgs!"

"We stepped on their face with a hobnail boot. . . ."

"Just a bunch of Junkyard Dawgs."

"Lindsay Scott!"

"Stick 'em with the Red Hats."

"Between the Hedges."

To the uninitiated, these phrases seem random, even a little strange. But to a true Georgia fan, they have a rich meaning that brings to mind a sunny Athens afternoon spent at Sanford Stadium, watching the Dawgs scrap and claw their way to another victory before a sea of red, as the Redcoat Band blares another rendition of "Glory, Glory" and new legends are born.

This is a program that virtually stands alone in the richness of its history and the passion of its fans. And with good reason. The images are unforgettable and too numerous to count. From the peerless running and throwing of Frank Sinkwich to the fearsome and relentless power/speed package of Herschel Walker; from the scrambling of Fran Tarkenton to the pinpoint passing of David Greene; from Wally Butts to Vince Dooley to Mark Richt—Georgia football is a legacy of greatness, a virtual way of life.

In this book, we've attempted to distill that tradition of greatness into the words and pictures that follow. It's a daunting task. Few programs inspire the loyalty and passion that Georgia football exacts from its fans, and with good reason.

But in the finest Georgia tradition, we've decided to hunker down and get it done. We hope you enjoy it.

TRADITIONS AND PAGEANTRY

The sights and sounds of Game Day in Athens create an unmatched spectacle, a glorious mix of tradition and color and pomp and pageantry. Here's a small sample of what makes Georgia football unique.

Uga

The family of Frank W. "Sonny" Seiler owns a line of white English bulldogs that has provided the University of Georgia with its mascot, Uga, since 1956. Uga VI currently serves the Bulldog faithful as an ever-present sideline inspiration. Uga wears a spiked collar emblematic of his status, and a letter jersey made of the same material as those worn by the players. He has been present at Heisman presentations and Final Fours, and he has graced the cover of *Sports Illustrated*. All of the deceased Ugas are buried in marble vaults on the grounds of Sanford Stadium with epitaphs inscribed in bronze.

Bulldogs Nickname

There has long been an assumption that the Georgia football team got its nickname "Bulldogs" from a historic connection with Yale. The first president of the University of Georgia, Abraham Baldwin, was a Yale man; many of the first buildings on the Athens campus were based on the designs of their Yale counterparts; and Georgia played Yale in football every year but one between 1923 and 1934. The truth is that in 1920, *Atlanta Journal* writer Morgan Blake suggested "Bulldogs" as a nickname for the Georgia team because "there is a certain dignity about a bulldog, as well as ferocity." Days later, *Atlanta Constitution* writer Cliff Wheatley used the nickname in his writeup of the scoreless tie with Virginia in Charlottesville, and the name has stuck ever since.

The "G" Helmet

Coach Vince Dooley instituted the oval "G" on the Georgia football helmets when he took over the program in 1964. Dooley's design was originally created by Anne Donaldson, wife of Georgia assistant coach John Donaldson, and similar to that of the Green Bay Packers, only with the appropriate colors of a black "G" on an oval white background on either side of the bright red helmet. Dooley also placed a white stripe over the top of the helmet.

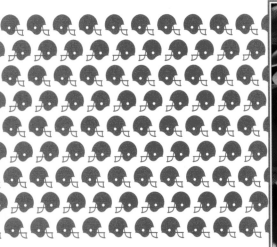

Silver Britches

"Go, You Silver Britches" is a Georgia football fan's battle cry, inspired by the silver pants introduced by Wally Butts, who became Georgia's head coach in 1939. The silver britches and red jerseys constituted a distinctive uniform. When Dooley took over as coach in 1964, he redesigned the uniforms to include white pants. He brought the silver britches back in 1980—the year his team posted a perfect record and won the national championship.

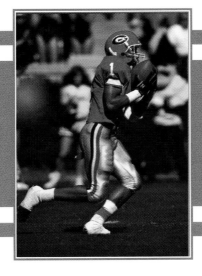

The Chapel Bell

When Georgia began playing football in the 1890s, the football field was located just yards from the chapel. After each victory in those early days, the freshmen were assigned the task of ringing the bell until midnight to celebrate. Today the chore is no longer a freshman responsibility, but students, fans and Athens residents still rush to the chapel after a victory to ring the bell.

Sanford Stadium

The three most prominent men in the history of Georgia football are coaches Wally Butts and Vince Dooley, and former university president Dr. Steadman Vincent Sanford, for whom Georgia's 92,058-seat football stadium is named. The stadium was opened in 1929 and dedicated with a 15-0 victory over Yale.

When any knowledgeable college football fan hears the expression "between the hedges," he knows the reference is to a football game in Sanford Stadium. Tradition has it that the phrase was coined by legendary sportswriter Grantland Rice, when he remarked about an upcoming contest that "the Bulldogs will have their opponents between the hedges." The English privet hedges that surround the playing field have been in place since the stadium opened, though at the time they were only a foot high and protected by a wooden fence.

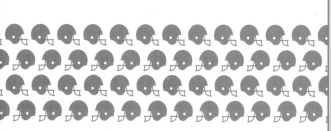

Redcoat Band

In 2004, the University of Georgia celebrated the 100th anniversary of the Redcoat Band, which operates under the auspices of the School of Music. Only about 30 percent of the 380-member contingent are music majors. The academically diverse group claims some of the highest grade-point averages on campus. Many of the Redcoats also belong to other musical organizations on campus, including three concert bands, two jazz bands and the Derbies Pep Band.

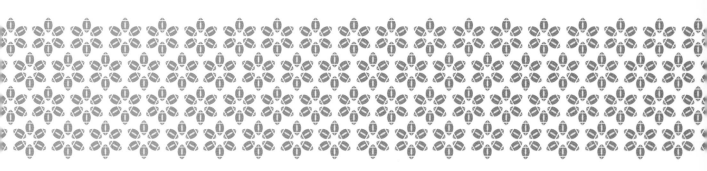

"Glory, Glory"

The school fight song, "Glory, Glory," is sung to the tune of the "Battle Hymn of the Republic." It has been heard at games dating back to the earliest years of the program, but in 1915, composer Hugh Hodgson arranged the tune into the form it is known today.

"Glory, Glory"

Glory, glory to old Georgia!

Glory, glory to old Georgia!

Glory, glory to old Georgia!

G-E-O-R-G-I-A

Glory, glory to old Georgia

Glory, glory to old Georgia

Glory, glory to old Georgia

G-E-O-R-G-I-A

Alma Mater

From the hills of Georgia's northland
Beams thy noble brow,
And the sons of Georgia rising
Pledge with sacred vow.

'Neath the pine tree's stately shadow
Spread thy riches rare,
And thy sons, dear Alma Mater
Will thy treasures share.

And thy daughters proudly join thee,
Take their rightful place,
Side by side into the future,
Equal dreams embrace.

Through the ages, Alma Mater,
Men will look to thee;
Thou the fairest of the Southland
Georgia's Varsity.

CHORUS:
Alma Mater, thee we'll honor,
True and loyal be, Ever crowned with praise and glory,
Georgia, hail to thee.

Larry Munson

Larry Munson is a game-day fixture whenever the Dawgs tee it up. Munson is entering his 40th year as the "Voice of the Dogs." Georgia football is not the only team to benefit from Munson's unique, captivating broadcasting style. He has also called Georgia basketball games, as well as both minor league and major league baseball.

Before he came to Athens, Munson called the shots for Vanderbilt football and basketball for 16 years, and he was the radio voice of the Nashville Vols of the Southern Baseball Association. He also has served as play-by-play man for Wyoming Cowboys football and basketball.

Without Munson at the mike, a Georgia football broadcast would be unrecognizable. His call of Verron Haynes' touchdown catch in the Dogs' 26-24 win at Tennessee in 2001— "We stepped on their face with a hobnail boot and broke their nose!"—has earned him national notoriety. But Munson is not a grand-stander; he is a professional, and one of the best, if not the best, in the business. And for this is his wide recognition well deserved.

THE GREATEST PLAYERS

Georgia football has seen its share of legends. The names are familiar to fans of college football, and for the fans of Georgia's rivals, they still bring a shiver of dread.

The Hall of Famers

BOB McWHORTER
Halfback, 1910-13

McWhorter was an All-Southern halfback all four years of his college career, and in 1913 he became the school's first All-American. He is the first person ever to captain both the football and baseball teams at UGa. Upon his graduation he turned down offers to play professional baseball in order to pursue a law career. In 1954, McWhorter was inducted in the College Football Hall of Fame.

VERNON "CATFISH" SMITH
End, 1929-31

Smith, a three-sport star at Georgia (football, basketball and baseball), was inducted into the College Football Hall of Fame in 1979. He was the star of Sanford Stadium's dedication game in 1929, when he scored all 15 points in Georgia's 15-0 win over Yale. Smith was an All-Southern end for three straight years, and went on to coach at Georgia, South Carolina and Ole Miss.

BILL HARTMAN

Fullback, 1935-37

Bill Hartman officially became a Hall of
Famer in 1984. He was a team captain and
All-American in 1937. He played professionally
for two seasons with the Washington Redskins,
and in one 1938 game, while subbing for an
injured Sammy Baugh, Hartman completed
13 consecutive passes against Brooklyn.
Later, he returned to Georgia as a member
of Wally Butts' coaching staff.

*"In 1936, we went up to New York and played a Fordham team that was
supposed to be heading to the Rose Bowl. They called their offensive line "The Seven Blocks of
Granite," and one of those blocks was Vince Lombardi. We were just a bunch of little Georgia
boys, and they had a marching band with about 100 people in it. I remember they kept playing
the song "California Here We Come" because the Rose Bowl was supposed to invite them after
the game. We led 7-0 for most of the game, but they came back and tied us 7-7. We knocked
them out of the Rose Bowl, though. We took the train back to Athens and got there about 5:30
Monday morning. There were over 10,000 people there to meet us."* BILL HARTMAN

FRANK SINKWICH
Halfback, 1940-42

Sinkwich became Georgia's first Heisman Trophy winner in 1942 and was inducted into the Hall of Fame in 1954. He captained the Bulldogs as a junior and senior. In the 1942 Orange Bowl, he threw touchdown passes of 61, 60 and 15 yards, ran for a 43-yard touchdown and piled up 382 total yards in Georgia's 40-26 win over TCU—all while playing with a broken jaw. In his Heisman year of '42, he led coach Wally Butts' Bulldogs to the national championship. Sadly, a knee injury suffered during a service football game ended his chances at a long pro career.

Frank Sinkwich vs. TCU in '42 Orange Bowl

L-R: Charley Trippi, Theron Sapp, Frank Sinkwich

"I came to Georgia a poor boy.
My first year in Athens I wore Coca-Cola work
pants and a T-shirt all the time. That's all I had.
But Georgia completely turned my life around. It
gave me a chance to excel in football, and I was
able to turn that into a very successful career in
professional football." CHARLEY TRIPPI

CHARLEY TRIPPI
Tailback, 1942, 1945-46

Trippi capped off his freshman season of 1942 with a Player of the Game performance in Georgia's 9-0 Rose Bowl win over UCLA, before spending the next two years in the service during World War II. As a senior in 1946, he led the Bulldogs to an 11-0 record and 20-10 Sugar Bowl win over North Carolina. That season he won the Maxwell Trophy as the nation's Most Valuable Player and was Heisman Trophy runner-up. He led the Chicago Cardinals to an NFL title as a rookie and was inducted into the College Football Hall of Fame in 1959.

"**I've lived in a lot of great places in my life,** and even though I was born in Pennsylvania, Athens and the University of Georgia will always feel like home. I never thought I could make it to the Hall of Fame, but I did, and it was because of the Georgia family. It was a team effort, and for that I will always be grateful."

Johnny Rauch

JOHNNY RAUCH
Quarterback, 1945-48

Rauch started all 45 games of his college career, including four straight bowl games, under Bulldog coach Wally Butts. He piloted two SEC championship teams, in 1946 and '48. The 1946 Bulldogs finished the season 11-0 and ranked third in the nation with Rauch calling signals. He threw for 4,044 career yards, which was then an NCAA record, and as a senior in 1948 he was named SEC Player of the Year. As a head coach of the Oakland Raiders from 1966 to 1968, he posted a record of 33-8-1, including a Super Bowl appearance in 1967. In 2003, he was enshrined in the College Football Hall of Fame.

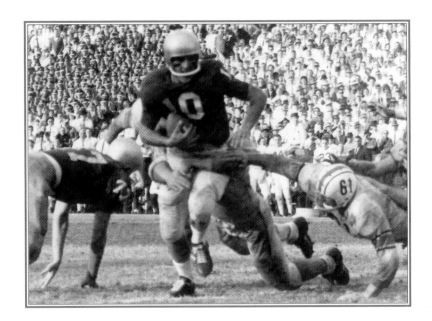

FRAN TARKENTON
Quarterback, 1958-60

Tarkenton is best remembered nationwide for his exploits as quarterback of the Minnesota Vikings of the NFL, but old-time SEC fans remember him as Georgia's All-America quarterback in 1960. As a junior, Tarkenton led the Bulldogs to the 1959 SEC championship and a 14-0 Orange Bowl victory over Missouri. His senior year, he led the conference in both passing yards (1,189) and total offense (1,274) before embarking on his 18-year NFL career. He is a member of both the College and Pro Football Halls of Fame.

BILL STANFILL
Defensive Tackle, 1966-68

Stanfill became Georgia's only Outland Trophy winner to date in 1968. A tall, nasty defensive tackle, Stanfill was a key component of the Bulldogs' 1966 and 1968 SEC championships. He was a star of three bowl teams following the 1966 (Cotton), 1967 (Liberty) and 1968 (Sugar) seasons. He was a consensus All-American as a senior, as well as an Academic All-American. He enjoyed an eight-year career in the NFL with the Miami Dolphins, was a starter on two Super Bowl champion teams (1972 and '73), and still holds the team career record for sacks with 67.5. Stanfill was elected to the College Football Hall of Fame in 1998.

"*He was a marvelous young kid with great athletic ability.*

He was the only player that could absolutely stop the triple option, at which time was unstoppable."
VINCE DOOLEY ON BILL STANFILL (ATLANTA JOURNAL-CONSTITUTION)

HERSCHEL WALKER
Tailback, 1980-82

Walker stands alongside Frank Sinkwich and Charley Trippi as the University of Georgia's all-time college football legends, but Walker probably had the greatest impact of all. During his three years as a Bulldog, he ran for 5,259 yards and led coach Vince Dooley's teams to a 33-3-1 record, three straight Sugar Bowl appearances, three straight SEC championships, and the 1980 national title. He set the NCAA freshman rushing record in 1980 with 1,616 yards and finished third in that year's Heisman voting. He was runner-up the following year and took home the hardware in 1982. He was a three-time consensus All-American and went into the Hall of Fame in 1999.

"He was the most productive football player that I've ever seen or coached. He was the most self-disciplined football player. No one has ever combined in one package the speed, the strength and the toughness and self-discipline that he combined."
VINCE DOOLEY ON HERSCHEL WALKER (ATLANTA JOURNAL-CONSTITUTION)

TERRY HOAGE
Rover, 1980-83

During Hoage's four years in coach Vince Dooley's defensive secondary, Georgia compiled a record of 43-4-1, captured three SEC crowns and one national title and made four major bowl appearances. Hoage was a consensus All-American as a junior and senior, and at the conclusion of his senior year in 1983 he finished fifth in the Heisman balloting, the highest ever for a defensive back up to that time. He played in the NFL for 13 years, including the 1992 season with the Washington Redskins Super Bowl champion team, and in 2000 he was inducted into the College Football Hall of Fame.

"It's amazing when I think of Terry and think of Herschel. Herschel was the most sought-after player in the country, and the least sought-after player was Terry Hoage. Both ended up being consensus All-Americans. Terry was absolutely brilliant. He just made one big play after another."

VINCE DOOLEY ON TERRY HOAGE (ATLANTA JOURNAL-CONSTITUTION)

KEVIN BUTLER
Placekicker, 1981-84

Butler was an All-American as a junior and senior and was All-SEC for all four of his years as a Bulldog. He holds the Georgia record for longest field goal (60 yards) and set an NCAA record with 27 multiple field goal games. Butler was instrumental in two SEC titles and four New Year's Day bowl appearances. His rookie year in the NFL was spent with the Super Bowl champion Bears, and he played professionally until 1997. He is arguably the greatest college placekicker ever, and is a 2001 Hall of Fame inductee.

"He was the greatest kicker we ever had. He was a great competitor and loved to play. Every time we'd go past the 50-yard line, he'd start walking in front of me. Sometimes, I'd have to get him out of the way." VINCE DOOLEY ON KEVIN BUTLER (ATLANTA JOURNAL-CONSTITUTION)

Other Georgia Greats

Far from a comprehensive list, this gallery of greats nonetheless gives a hint of the scope of the Georgia football tradition.

JAKE SCOTT
Defensive Back, 1966-68

Scott made his name nationally as an All-Pro for the Miami Dolphins, but his college career was equally impressive. A first-team All-SEC selection in 1967 and 1968 and an All-American in 1968, Scott intercepted 10 passes for 175 yards and two TDs in Georgia's 1968 SEC title drive. Scott also led the SEC in punt returns in 1968. In 1982, Scott was selected to the All-Time SEC team by the SEC skywriters.

"When you think of talent, you think of Jake. *I don't know that we had a better talented player or one that loved the game more. Jake studied the game as much as anybody, though a lot of people did not realize that."*
VINCE DOOLEY ON JAKE SCOTT (ATLANTA JOURNAL-CONSTITUTION)

GEORGE PATTON
Defensive Tackle, 1964-66

The first dominant player of the Vince Dooley era at Georgia, Patton defined toughness. Patton scored a 56-yard TD against defending national champion Alabama as a senior to help the Bulldogs to their 18-17 upset victory. Fittingly, he was named permanent captain of the 1966 SEC Champion Bulldogs. Patton was a two-time All-American (1965-66).

"He helped me stay employed that first year that I came. George was a quarterback, and we were looking to move people with any kind of speed, so we moved him to tackle. You don't find many quarterbacks that can play tackle, but he did and played it with great confidence and with great leadership."

VINCE DOOLEY ON GEORGE PATTON (ATLANTA JOURNAL-CONSTITUTION)

BEN ZAMBIASI
Linebacker, 1974-77

When you think of the Junkyard Dawgs, one name typically comes to mind: Ben Zambiasi. A three-time all-SEC performer at linebacker, Zambiasi posted 467 career tackles, including 165 in the Dawgs' 1977 Sugar Bowl season. Zambiasi went on to a great career in the Canadian Football League and is a member of the CFL Hall of Fame.

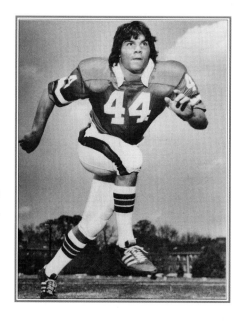

"He was another one of those relentless players. He would get so worked up before a game when I would talk to the team before sending them out. The more I'd talk, the more fired up Ben got. The more fired up Ben got, the more fired up I got and the better job I did." VINCE DOOLEY ON BEN ZAMBIASI (ATLANTA JOURNAL-CONSTITUTION)

SCOTT WOERNER
Defensive Back, 1977-80

Woerner possessed more heart than talent, but he was pretty talented, too. The defensive back and return specialist made a huge mark on the 1980 national championship team, earning All-America honors after intercepting five passes. He also led the nation in punt returns and set a school record of 15.7 yards per return.

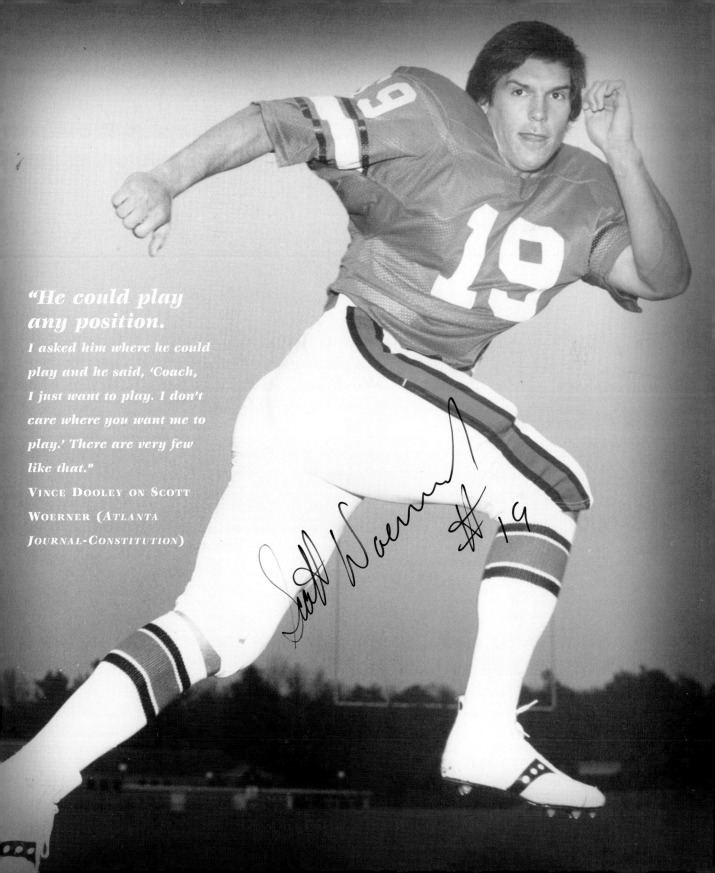

"He could play any position. I asked him where he could play and he said, 'Coach, I just want to play. I don't care where you want me to play.' There are very few like that."

VINCE DOOLEY ON SCOTT WOERNER (ATLANTA JOURNAL-CONSTITUTION)

JIMMY PAYNE,

Defensive Tackle, 1978-82

Payne was the quintessential pass rusher. The All-SEC defensive tackle had 85 tackles and seven sacks for the Bulldogs in 1981. Knee problems prevented Payne from playing in the NFL, and tragically, he died of cancer in Athens in 1998.

"He was an All-America pass rusher. He could have played other positions. He could have been a tight end. He and Freddie Gilbert were the George Patton and Bill Stanfill of the 1980s." VINCE DOOLEY ON JIMMY PAYNE (ATLANTA JOURNAL-CONSTITUTION)

KNOX CULPEPPER

Linebacker, 1981-84

Culpepper, whose father, Knox Sr., was also a great player at Georgia, was a tackle machine during his tenure. A two-time All-SEC linebacker, the undersized but relentless Culpepper was the captain of Georgia's 1984 team.

"He was another one of those overachievers. Knox might hold the tackles record for many, many years. He was a Georgia man through and through because he inherited his Georgia heritage from his father, who also was a Georgia player." VINCE DOOLEY ON KNOX CULPEPPER (ATLANTA JOURNAL-CONSTITUTION)

GARRISON HEARST
Running Back, 1990-92

A worthy heir to the running back tradition established by players like Herschel Walker and Rodney Hampton—his immediate predecessor in the Bulldog backfield—Hearst was an All-SEC and All-American running back in 1992. That year, Hearst was honored with the Doak Walker Award, given annually to college football's best running back.

"We did finish off that season (1992) with a good win over Ohio State (21-14) in the Citrus Bowl. Man, did they talk a lot of junk. They thought they were the team of the century because they were from the Big Ten. They thought they shouldn't have to play a team like Georgia. But we showed them why the SEC is the best conference in the country."
GARRISON HEARST

ERIC ZEIER

Quarterback, 1991-94

Zeier was Georgia's greatest passing quarterback of the 20th century, and one of the greatest anywhere. The records he set are too numerous for an exhaustive list, but they include 11,153 career passing yards. In all he concluded his stay at Athens with 67 school and 18 SEC records. Against Southern Miss in his junior year, he completed 30 of 47 attempts for 544 yards and four touchdowns. As a senior in 1994, the American Football Coaches Association named him to its All-America first team.

"The bottom line for me has always been this: we didn't win as many football games as we would have liked at Georgia, and we didn't reach all of our goals, but even if I had never played football, Georgia is where I would have gone to college. I made friendships there and established relationships that will be with me for the rest of my life. You can't put a price on that." ERIC ZEIER

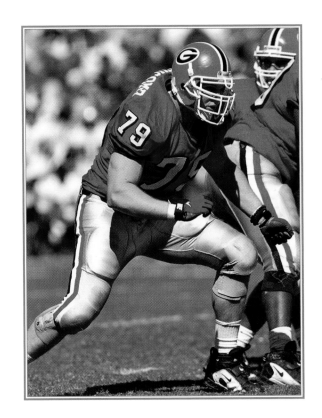

MATT STINCHCOMB

Offensive Tackle, 1995-98

Stinchcomb was a road-grading tackle who earned All-America honors in 1997 and 1998. Perhaps an even greater source of pride for Stinchcomb is the fact that he was also a two-time academic All-American who graduated with a 3.96 grade point average.

"Nobody ever noticed, but when I would take my unofficial visits to other schools (during the recruiting process), I would always do it on the Saturday they were playing Georgia."
MATT STINCHCOMB

CHAMP BAILEY
Defensive Back, 1996-98

Bailey may have been the most versatile player in Georgia football history. He was a participant in more than 1,000 plays in 1998 as a cornerback, wide receiver and special-teams player. Bailey was a first-round pick of the Washington Redskins in 1999.

"I love Georgia. I grew up a Bulldog fan, and I always wanted to be a Bulldog. But the experience was everything I hoped it would be. Georgia was the perfect fit for me, and I felt like I had a great career there. I wouldn't change it for anything in the world." CHAMP BAILEY

DAVID GREENE
Quarterback, 2001-04

Of all the records Eric Zeier broke, most now belong to David Greene. In his four years as a starter, Greene threw and completed more passes (849 of 1,440) for more yards (11,528) and more touchdowns (72) than anyone else in Georgia history. He started all 51 games of his career, led the Bulldogs to the 2002 SEC championship as a sophomore and exited with more wins as a starting quarterback than anyone else in NCAA history.

"The great thing about winning the SEC Championship was that I was born in 1982, and it was hard for me to believe that Georgia had not won a championship for as long as I was alive. I know we can't wipe out all the suffering the Georgia people had to go through in those 20 years, but I am glad I was part of the team that got us back there."
DAVID GREENE

DAVID POLLACK

Defensive End, 2001-04

The last time Pollack wore a Georgia uniform, he was finishing his college career with a flourish, sacking Wisconsin quarterback John Stocco three times in the 2005 Outback Bowl. Pollack made himself at home in opponents' backfields, with 58 tackles for losses over his four years in Athens. He holds the UGa record with 36 career sacks. Pollack was All-SEC and All-America his final three years, and as a 2004 senior he won the Lombardi Award as the College Lineman of the Year.

"There's just something special about being a Bulldog.

That's why I had to stay for my senior year." DAVID POLLACK

THE GREAT COACHES

Georgia has been blessed with some of the game's greatest tacticians, motivators and leaders. Three names rise to the top of the list.

Wally Butts

In 1938, Wally Butts came to Georgia to coach the ends under one-year head coach Joel Hunt. The following year, Butts took over the program as head coach and stayed for 22 years. The Bulldogs had experienced success on the football field earlier, but they became a national power during Butts' coaching tenure. Butts took Georgia to its first bowl game, the 1942 Orange Bowl, and then seven more bowl appearances after that. He also coached the Bulldogs to two national championships, in 1942 and '46, and four SEC titles. Among his greatest players were 1942 Heisman Trophy winner Frank Sinkwich and 1946 Maxwell Award winner Charley Trippi. NFL Hall of Fame quarterback Fran Tarkenton is another of Butts' pupils. At the time of his resignation after the 1960 campaign, the "Little Round Man" sported a record of 140-86-9.

"Coach Butts was a hard man to know, and I can't say I ever really knew him. But I can say this: the man was a genius when it came to the passing game."
FRAN TARKENTON

WALLY BUTTS YEAR BY YEAR AT GEORGIA

YEAR	RECORD	BOWL
1939	5-6-0	
1940	5-4-1	
1941	9-1-1	Orange
1942	11-1-0	Rose
1943	6-4-0	
1944	7-3-0	
1945	9-2-0	Oil
1946	11-0-0	Sugar
1947	7-4-1	Gator
1948	9-2-0	Orange
1949	4-6-1	
1950	6-3-3	
1951	5-5-0	
1952	7-4-0	
1953	3-8-0	
1954	6-3-1	
1955	4-6-0	
1956	3-6-1	
1957	3-7-0	
1958	4-6-0	
1959	10-1-0	
1960	6-4-0	

"Everything that I ever became in football I owe to Georgia and to Coach Butts. He could be as tough as a football coach could be, but each one of us knew that if we were ever in trouble we could go to Coach Butts. He did so many good things that nobody ever knew about. There is only one man I respected more, and that was my father."* JOHNNY RAUCH

Vince Dooley

During Vince Dooley's quarter century as head coach (1964-88), the Bulldogs posted a losing record just once. Dooley's teams were known as tough, fundamentally sound and highly motivated. He is the most successful coach in school history, having posted a record of 201-77-10, with a consensus national championship in 1980 and a piece of another in 1968. His teams also won six SEC titles and participated in 20 bowl games. Dooley was named National Coach of the Year in 1980 and is a seven-time SEC Coach of the Year. During the Dooley years, Georgia produced 1982 Heisman Trophy winner Herschel Walker and 1968 Outland Trophy winner Bill Stanfill. He is one of just 10 coaches in NCAA Division I history with 200 career wins, and in 1994 he was inducted into the College Football Hall of Fame.

VINCE DOOLEY YEAR BY YEAR AT GEORGIA

YEAR	RECORD	BOWL
1964	7-3-1	Sun
1965	6-4-0	
1966	10-1-0	Cotton
1967	7-4-0	Liberty
1968	8-1-2	Sugar
1969	5-5-1	Sun
1970	5-5-0	
1971	11-1-0	Gator
1972	7-4-0	
1973	7-4-1	Peach
1974	6-6-0	Tangerine
1975	9-3-0	Cotton
1976	10-2-0	Sugar
1977	5-6-0	
1978	9-2-1	Bluebonnet
1979	6-5-0	
1980	12-0-0	Sugar
1981	10-2-0	Sugar
1982	11-1-0	Sugar
1983	10-1-1	Cotton
1984	7-4-1	Citrus
1985	7-3-2	Sun
1986	8-4-0	Hall of Fame
1987	9-3-0	Liberty
1988	9-3-0	Gator

*"**At Georgia, we always worked very hard** to build a reputation that our players could embrace and our opponents would have to acknowledge. And that reputation was this:*

- *When you play Georgia, you better buckle up your chin strap because you're going to be in a battle.*
- *When you play Georgia, we are going to hit you for 60 minutes, and the game is going to go down to the wire.*
- *We may not win, but if you play for Georgia, then you better be laying it on the line every play in every game. If you do that, then we'll win our fair share.*

When I think about what it means to be a Bulldog, I always go back to tenacity and loyalty. Georgia people are committed to their state, their university and their football team. Once you become a part of the Georgia family, you have a support structure that is second to none." VINCE DOOLEY

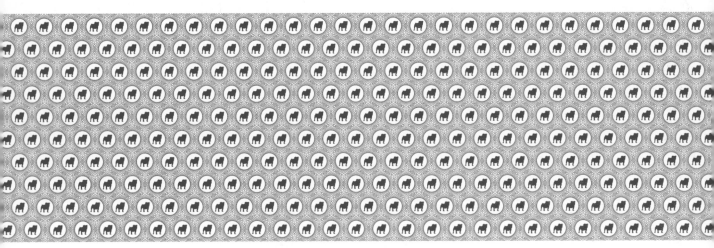

"His work habits are extraordinary. He does things until he does them the right way." BILL LEWIS, DEFENSIVE COORDINATOR UNDER VINCE DOOLEY

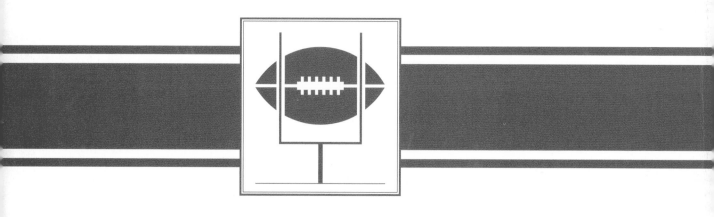

Mark Richt

Mark Richt became head coach of the Georgia Bulldogs on Dec. 26, 2000 after 11 years as quarterbacks coach and offensive coordinator at Florida State. In his four years at the helm in Athens, Richt's teams have accumulated the sixth-best record in the nation with 42-10. Under Richt's coaching, the Bulldogs have claimed two SEC Eastern Division championships (2002 and '03), and in 2002 they claimed the conference crown. Richt's Georgia teams have yet to finish a season outside the national rankings, and have landed in the Top 10 in each of the last three years, including a third-place finish in 2002. The Bulldogs are currently riding a three-game winning streak in postseason action with Richt in command. Two of the players from Richt's first four years—quarterback David Greene and defensive end David Pollack—will be remembered as legends.

MARK RICHT YEAR BY YEAR AT GEORGIA

YEAR	RECORD	BOWL
2001	8-4	Music City
2002	13-1	Sugar
2003	11-3	Capital One
2004	10-2	Outback

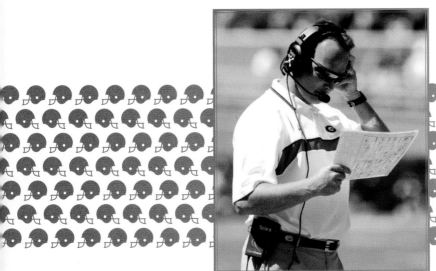

"The thing that has struck me the most in my time here is the passion of the Georgia people. The love fans have for Georgia is felt very deeply, and it is passed on from generation to generation. That love for this program and this university is why Georgia is such a great place."* MARK RICHT*

BULLDOG SUPERLATIVES

Georgia football history is littered with moments of greatness—national championships won, great games played, superior individual efforts, memorable upsets and more. Here is a small sample of that record of achievement.

The Championships

NATIONAL CHAMPIONSHIPS
1942

The 1942 Georgia team produced two of the greatest players ever to wear the red and black, legends of the college game: Frank Sinkwich and Charley Trippi. Along with All-America end George Poschner and All-SEC guard Walter Ruark, among others, coach Wally Butts had assembled the nation's premier team that year. The '42 Bulldogs stormed to nine straight victories, mostly of the no-doubt variety, right out of the gate. In the Alabama contest, Georgia trailed 10-0 after three quarters, whereupon Sinkwich went to work, passing his team to the 21-10 win. He connected with a well-covered Poschner in the end zone for the go-ahead touchdown and the Bulldogs coasted from there. The following week, Georgia annihilated Florida 75-0. Butts' club hit a bump in the road with a 27-13 loss to Auburn to drop to 9-1 but got back on track with a 34-0 thumping of 9-0 Georgia Tech in the regular-season finale. Georgia went on to whitewash UCLA 9-0 in the Rose Bowl, Sinkwich won the Heisman Trophy and Butts' Bulldogs were awarded the national title by no fewer than six of the NCAA recognized polling systems.

SEC CHAMPIONSHIPS

YEAR	OVERALL	CONFERENCE	COACH
1942	11-1-0	6-1-0	Wally Butts
1946	11-0-0	5-0-0	Wally Butts
1948	9-2-0	6-0-0	Wally Butts
1959	10-1-0	7-0-0	Wally Butts
1966	10-1-0	6-0-0	Vince Dooley
1968	8-1-2	5-0-1	Vince Dooley
1976	10-2-0	5-1-0	Vince Dooley
1980	12-0-0	6-0-0	Vince Dooley
1981	10-2-0	6-0-0	Vince Dooley
1982	11-1-0	6-0-0	Vince Dooley
2002	13-1-0	8-1-0	Mark Richt

1980

The most compelling image of the 1980 Georgia season is, and always will remain, Lindsay Scott's run with a short Buck Belue pass for a 93-yard touchdown to snatch a 26-21 victory from the jaws of defeat in the Florida game. The true significance of the play was that it rescued a perfect season and a consensus national championship for coach Vince Dooley's Bulldogs. There were a few close calls besides the Florida game, including a 16-15 squeaker in the opener at Tennessee, but Texas A&M was dispatched 42-0 the following Saturday, and there were consecutive midseason shutouts over Vanderbilt (41-0) and Kentucky (27-0). Georgia prevailed in a battle of top 10 teams with a 13-10 win over South Carolina to shoot to No. 2 nationally, then seized the top spot after the Florida game and never let it go. The regular season concluded with workmanlike wins over Auburn and Georgia Tech. In the Sugar Bowl, freshman Herschel Walker scored twice in a 17-10 win over Notre Dame, and at 12-0 there was no disputing Georgia's claim to the title. Walker, cornerback Scott Woerner and kicker Rex Robinson were All-Americans.

The 1980 National Champion
Georgia Bulldogs

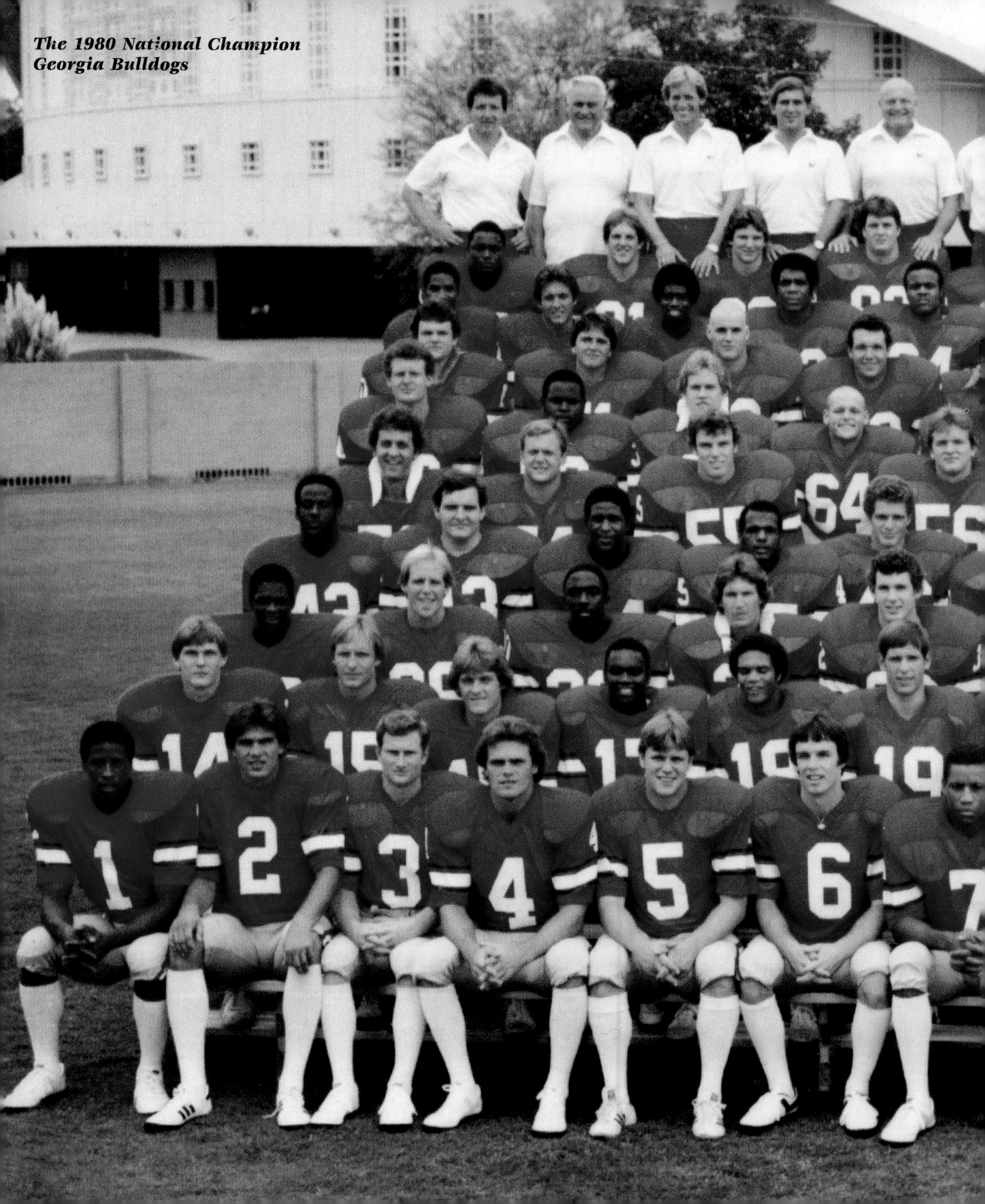

Great Bulldog Teams

1927

The 1927 Georgia team, the "Dream and Wonder Team" of coach George Woodruff, stormed through its first nine opponents undefeated. In Game 2, the Bulldogs defeated Yale for the first time in five tries. They then proceeded to shut out their next five opponents. They took a No. 1 national ranking into the season finale at Georgia Tech. The game was played in a quagmire following a 24-hour rain, neutralizing Georgia's superior speed, and Tech prevailed 12-0. The 1927 Bulldogs, who surrendered a grand total of 35 points all year, were led by not one but two All-America ends: Chick Shiver and Tom Nash.

1946

Georgia finished the 1946 season 11-0 but finished ranked third in the nation behind Notre Dame and Army, who had played each other to a scoreless tie that year. Georgia, meanwhile, was not seriously challenged once all season, defeating Alabama 14-0, Florida 33-14 and Auburn 41-0. The Bulldogs closed out the regular season with a 35-7 thumping of Georgia Tech and took care of Charlie "Choo-Choo" Justice and North Carolina in the Sugar Bowl 20-0. Charley Trippi was the star of the show for the 1946 Bulldogs. It was Trippi's senior season, and he led the SEC in scoring with 84 points. He compiled 1,366 yards of total offense, won the Maxwell Award as the nation's Most Valuable Player and was Heisman Trophy runner-up. Quarterback John Rauch, end Joe Tereshinski, tackle Jack Bush and guard Herb St. John were All-SEC in '46.

1968

Despite opening the season with a 17-17 tie at Tennessee and playing Houston to a 10-10 deadlock later in the season, the Bulldogs entered the Sugar Bowl undefeated at 8-0-2. The regular season concluded with victories over Florida (51-0), Auburn (17-3) and Georgia Tech (47-8). That the Bulldogs emerged with a piece of the national championship (from the Litkenhous poll) despite a 16-2 New Year's Day loss to Arkansas is a tribute to one of the all-time great defenses. Tackle Bill Stanfill and safety Jake Scott were All-Americans, and Stanfill captured the Outland Trophy that season. Second-team All-SEC quarterback Mike Cavan directed the attack.

1981

Vince Dooley's Bulldogs opened the 1981 season hoping to repeat as national champions. A 44-0 victory over Tennessee got the season off to a rousing start, but a turnover-plagued performance in Game 3 against Clemson led to a 13-3 loss. That was followed by eight straight wins to finish the regular season 10-1. Quarterback Buck Belue, tailback Herschel Walker and company sailed into New Orleans with a No. 2 national ranking to take on Pittsburgh in the Sugar Bowl. A last-minute loss, 24-20, dropped the Bulldogs to sixth in the final rankings. Besides Walker, who ran for 1,891 yards that fall, and Belue, other Bulldogs who crowded the All-SEC rosters that fall were wide receiver Lindsay Scott, defensive tackle Jimmy Payne, Rover Terry Hoage and placekicker Kevin Butler, among others.

1982

It was Herschel Walker's final year in Athens. At the end of the regular season, Georgia was 11-0 and had been ranked No. 1 in the nation for the last five weeks. The campaign closed with wins over Florida (44-0), Auburn (19-14) and Georgia Tech (38-18). The win over Auburn that clinched the SEC title was punctuated by Larry Munson's memorable call: "Hunker down! . . . Oh, look at the Sugar falling out of the sky." But the Bulldogs fell to Penn State 27-23 in a Sugar Bowl matchup that decided that year's national title. Walker ran for 1,752 yards and 17 touchdowns and won the Heisman Trophy. Defensive tackle Jimmy Payne and rover Terry Hoage joined Walker as All-Americans that fall, with center Wayne Radloff, guard Guy McIntyre, kicker Kevin Butler, and linebacker Tommy Thurson swelling the All-SEC ranks.

1983

Defensive end and captain Freddie Gilbert, two-time consensus All-America defensive back Terry Hoage and kicker Kevin Butler were the stars of the 1983 Georgia team that had been bested only once all season—13–7 to Auburn. A 16-16 early season tie at Clemson also marred the record. No one gave Georgia much of a chance against undefeated, untied, second-ranked Texas in the Cotton Bowl. But Vince Dooley's Dawgs scored a late touchdown to win the game 10-9. Top-ranked Nebraska also lost that day, but Georgia would finish no higher than fourth.

2002

Coach Mark Richt was in his second year at the helm in Athens, David Greene was in his second year at quarterback and defensive end David Pollack was enjoying the finest year of his college career. Greene threw for a hair under 3,000 yards and 22 touchdowns that season, Pollack racked up 23.5 tackles for loss and 14 sacks, and the two were fast becoming legends. The 2002 Bulldogs won more games (13) than any other football team in school history and captured their first SEC title in 20 years. Only a 20-13 loss to Florida kept Georgia out of the national championship game. After defeating Arkansas 30-3 in the SEC title game and Florida State 26-13 in the Sugar Bowl, Georgia came away with a third-place national ranking in the final poll.

Greatest Games

Georgia vs. Alabama in Atlanta, Oct. 31, 1942

Georgia won the national championship in 1942 but had its hands full with Alabama in a game played on Atlanta's Grant Field. Two backfield immortals—Frank Sinkwich and Charley Trippi—graced the Bulldog roster that year, and this was Sinkwich's Heisman-winning season. The Crimson Tide had bottled up the All-American for three quarters before he broke loose in the fourth. Trailing 10-0, Sinkwich completed 11 of 13 passes to start the final stanza, and connected with All-SEC end George Poschner in the corner of the end zone to cut 'Bama's lead to 10-7. The Bulldogs quickly regained possession of the ball and Sinkwich again passed his team to within striking distance. He then threaded the needle to a tightly covered Poschner in the end zone for a 14-10 lead. The Bulldogs later scored on a fumble recovery, and what had been a 10-0 fourth-quarter deficit turned into a 21-10 victory, and the national title train stayed on track.

Georgia vs. Texas in 1984 Cotton Bowl

Georgia entered the 1984 Cotton Bowl against 11-0, second-ranked Texas as heavy underdogs. Both defenses were expected to show up, and they did not disappoint. The first half ended 3-3. The Longhorns tacked on two more field goals in the third period, but neither team crossed the goal line until the game's waning moments. Longhorn Craig Curry fumbled a punt, Bulldog sophomore Gary Moss pounced on the ball and the Dogs were in business at the Texas 23. On third down, Georgia quarterback John Lastinger took the ball around right end 17 yards to paydirt. All-America placekicker Kevin Butler scored the decisive point to put the Bulldogs up 10-9. The UGA defense stifled the Longhorns on their last possession, with Kenny Sims and Ed Moore each recording a sack, and the huge upset was in the books. And Georgia passed Texas in the final national ranking, finishing fourth to the Longhorns' fifth.

Georgia vs. Florida, Nov. 8, 1980

In 1980, Georgia was on the fast track to a national title, but the express was almost derailed in the Florida game. It was Herschel Walker's freshman year at tailback; Buck Belue directed the attack at quarterback. The Gators held a 21-20 lead, and Georgia was backed up on its own 7-yard line, third-and-10, with 1:35 to play. Belue took the snap, rolled to his right and, thanks to a key block by Nat Hudson, had time to find Lindsay Scott crossing underneath the Gator secondary. He hit Scott in stride and the speedy wideout did the rest, scoring on a 93-yard catch and run that remains the most memorable play in Georgia history. Georgia won the game 26-21, went on to beat Notre Dame in the Sugar Bowl and was crowned national champion of 1980.

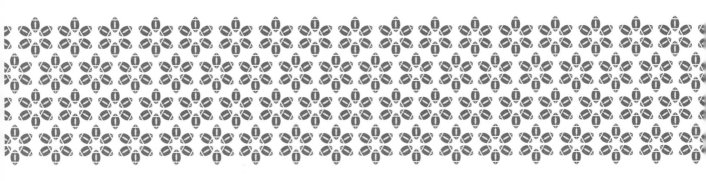

Greatest Single-Game Performances

 End **Vernon "Catfish" Smith** was an All-American in 1931, but his is best remembered for his performance in the 1929 game against Yale. Georgia had come out on the short end in five of the six games the two schools had played, and the Bulldogs from New Haven, Conn., were invited down for a game to dedicate newly constructed Sanford Stadium. In that game, Georgia won 15-0, and Smith scored all 15 points. First, he recovered a blocked punt for a touchdown and kicked the extra point. Later, he ran Yale's legendary Hall of Famer Albie Booth out of bounds for a safety. And finally, he caught a long touchdown pass.

Frank Sinkwich won the 1942 Heisman Trophy, and it may have been his performance in the Orange Bowl following the 1941 season that put his name out there. Playing with a broken jaw he suffered in the South Carolina game, Sinkwich set an Orange Bowl record with 382 total yards. He threw touchdown passes of 61, 60 and 15 yards, and ran 43 yards for another. It was the greatest performance in postseason history to that time. And oh, by the way, Georgia won 40-26.

L-R: Charley Trippi, Theron Sapp, Frank Sinkwich

Over its long, illustrious football history, the University of Georgia has retired exactly four jerseys. Three belonged to legends Frank Sinkwich, Charley Trippi and Herschel Walker. The fourth was worn by a good football player but hardly a household name: **Theron Sapp**. In 1957, Georgia was enduring what its fans referred to as "The Drought," an eight-game losing streak against Georgia Tech. The Bulldogs were 2-7 and assured of a third-straight losing season when they traveled to Atlanta to take on the Techsters in the season finale. The game was scoreless in the third quarter when Sapp, playing linebacker, pounced on a Georgia Tech fumble at midfield. On offense, Sapp went to fullback and bulled his way for a first down at the 37. Later in the drive he picked up 25 yards on six straight carries into the middle of the line. On 4th-and-goal at the 1, he scored the game's only touchdown against a Tech defense that hadn't allowed a rushing touchdown at home all season. The Bulldogs won 7-0 and Sapp had

his number retired upon his graduation after the following year. He enjoyed a solid career and was All-SEC in 1958, but he will always be remembered as "The Drought Breaker."

In 1959, **Charley Britt** played safety for coach Wally Butts' 10-1 SEC champions. In the Florida game, he came off the bench for an ailing Fran Tarkenton at quarterback. He quickly led the Bulldogs to an early touchdown, then he fielded a Florida quick-kick and returned it 27 yards to the Gator 37. Moments later he connected with receiver Bobby Towns for a 34-yard touchdown pass. In the second quarter he caught Florida's Bobby Joe Green from behind with a touchdown-saving tackle after chasing him practically the entire length of the field. In the second half, with Florida knocking on the door at the Georgia 10, Britt intercepted a pass in the end zone and raced 100 yards for a touchdown to preserve a 21-10 win.

Theron Sapp

Great Moments

The Comeback

The 1978 edition of the Georgia Bulldogs provided a season-long lesson in heart. The 9-2-1 season had many highlights, including a huge season from SEC Player of the Year Willie McClendon. There was also the incident at LSU, when Uga barked at Mike the tiger prior to the game, sending the great cat slinking back in his cage and inspiring coach Vince Dooley to rush to the dressing room and announce, "Let's go men. We've got 'em tonight." But the greatest moment came in the season finale. Against the hated Georgia Tech Yellow Jackets, the Bulldogs fell behind 20-0 before mounting a stirring, epic comeback. The keys: a 72-yard Scott Woerner punt return and game-winning-drive heroics by a freshman quarterback named Buck Belue. A Belue-to-Amp Arnold two-point conversion in the game's waning moments sealed the 29-28 Bulldog victory.

Herschel's Coming-Out Party

For many, the modern era of Georgia football began when Herschel Walker bulldozed over Tennessee's Bill Bates on the first touchdown run of his storied career in Georgia's thrilling 16-15 win over the Vols in Neyland Stadium that opened the 1980 National Championship season. Here's how Larry Munson called Herschel's coming-out party:

"Tennessee leading 15-2, the crowd roaring against Georgia trying to make them drop it so they can't hear. We hand it off to Herschel, there's a hole, 5, 10, 12, he's running over people! Oh, you Herschel Walker! My God almighty, he ran right through two men, Herschel ran right over two men, they had him dead away inside the 9. Herschel Walker went 16 yards, he drove right over those orange shirts and is just driving and running with those big thighs. My God, a freshman!"

The Kick

Kevin Butler's range was seemingly limitless. But no one could have imagined what Butler would do to Clemson in the classic 1984 Bulldogs-Tigers matchup. Here's how Munson saw things that day as Butler's 60-yard field goal beat Clemson 26-23:

"So we'll try and kick one 100,000 miles, we hold it on our own 49$\frac{1}{2}$, 60 yards plus a foot, and Butler kicks a long one, Butler kicks a long one, Oh my God! Oh my God! Oh my God! . . . The stadium is worse than bonkers. Eleven seconds left and I can't believe what I saw. This is ungodly!"

The Drive

All seemed lost as Tennessee took a late lead over Georgia in the classic 2001 encounter. But the Dawgs' David Greene had other ideas. He found Damien Gary and Randy McMichael on one huge pass play after another, setting up the game-winner to little-used fullback Verron Haynes on a little dump pass over the middle—Georgia 26, Tennessee 24. Here's Munson's immortal call, which will be remembered as long as Georgia plays football:

"Touchdown! We threw it to Haynes. We just stuffed them with five seconds left! My God almighty, it's 26-24! We just stepped on their face with a hobnail boot and broke their nose. We just crushed their faces!"

The Touchdown

Perhaps the greatest chapter in the story of the South's Oldest Rivalry was written in 2002. Georgia, fighting for an SEC Eastern Division championship, faced a 21-17 deficit at Auburn (after trailing by 11 at the half) with time winding down. After converting a fourth-and-15, the Bulldogs faced a fourth-and-10 at the Auburn 19 with 90 seconds left when quarterback David Greene lofted a pass toward the corner of the end zone, where relative unknown Michael Johnson waited. One well-timed jump later, and Johnson had his slice of SEC immortality, while Georgia had its first championship in 20 years.

Here's how Greene describes it: *"When you think about the touchdown play to Michael Johnson, you have to think that it was meant for us to win that night. We were down to our last play, and I had been taught to get the ball there and give the receiver a chance to make the play. Michael fought for the ball, the defender slipped a little bit, and he timed his jump perfectly. There were a million ways that play could have turned out, but we made it, and it put us in position to win the SEC Championship.*

"I've heard that people will be talking about that play 20 or 30 years from now just like they talk about the other great plays in Georgia history. That really blows my mind. Because at this time in our lives, those of us who play don't realize what is taking place. We think we're just out there playing ball, but at the same time we're really making history."

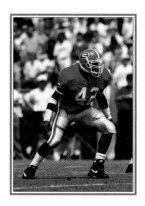

THE RIVALRIES

Three great rivalries have helped define Georgia football and have given fans many of their greatest memories.

Florida

It's called "The World's Largest Outdoor Cocktail Party." The festivities surrounding the football game almost overshadow the game itself. RVs begin arriving early in the week and don't start clearing out until Sunday.

Every year since 1933 the Florida-Georgia game has been held in Jacksonville, Fla., with the exception of a two-year home-and-home hiatus in 1994 and '95, during the renovation of its venue from the Gator Bowl to AllTel Stadium.

The two schools squared off for the first time in 1915, and they have played every year since 1926 with the exception of 1943, when the Gators did not field a team during the height of World War II. Of the last 42 matchups, half of them have been decided by seven or fewer points.

The first meeting in the Gator Bowl was played before 21,000 fans, compared to the more than 80,000 that throng to the event these days. In that 1933 contest, coach Harry Mehre's Georgia team knocked Florida out of the Southeastern Conference race by a score of 14-0.

In 1964, Georgia placekicker Bobby Etter scooped up a fumbled field-goal snap from the turf and ran it in for a touchdown with less than two minutes to play for a 14-7 Bulldog win. The following year, Gator quarterback Steve Spurrier moved his team 78 yards in two plays for a late score and a 14-10 Florida victory.

In 1966, Spurrier won the Heisman Trophy, but not the Georgia game. The Gators held a 10-3 lead at halftime, but Georgia's defense, led by tackle Bill Stanfill, put the clamps on Spurrier in the second half and went on to a 27-10 victory.

In 1976, Florida was on the verge of its first ever SEC championship, with Georgia standing in the way. The Gators took a 27-13 lead into the locker room at intermission, and still held on to a 27-20 lead when they decided to go for a first down on fourth-and-1 at their own 29. Florida coach Doug Dickey's "fourth and dumb" call didn't work, as Georgia safety Johnny Henderson threw the Gator ball carrier to the ground for a loss. The Bulldogs got the ball with a short field and scored. And they scored again and again, and won the game 41-27.

But the greatest fireworks came in the 1975 and 1980 clashes. In '75 Georgia was backed up on its own 20, trailing 7-3 with 3:24 left in the game. Bulldog tight end Richard Appleby took the ball on an apparent end-around then stopped, planted and threw deep to flanker Gene Washington, who was open downfield. The 80-yard touchdown play gave the Bulldogs a 10-7 victory.

In 1980, Georgia entered the contest with a No. 2 national ranking. The Bulldogs' shot at the national championship was on the line, with Florida leading 21-20 and 1:35 to play. Georgia had the ball on its own 7-yard line. 3rd-and-10. Quarterback Buck Belue took the snap, rolled to his right, got a great block from Nat Hudson and hit wide receiver Lindsay Scott underneath the Gators' secondary. Scott shook off tacklers and raced to the end zone for the 93-yard touchdown that won the game 26-21. The Bulldogs finished the season as national champions.

The "World's Largest Outdoor Cocktail Party" is more than a daylong binge for 80,000 fans. It's usually a pretty important football game. Here's a look back at the greatest of all cocktail parties.

Score: Georgia 26, Florida 21

Date: Nov. 8, 1980

Details: Georgia had moved up to No. 2 in the nation after a 13-10 win over South Carolina in a battle of top 10 teams. But the following week, it appeared that the Dawgs' dream run was over. Georgia trailed Florida 21-20 with 1:04 to play facing third and 10 from its own 7-yard line.

If you know anything about college football, you know what happened next. Buck Belue hit a streaking Lindsay Scott over the middle, and Scott scooted into the end zone to complete a miraculous 93-yard touchdown (Scott's only TD reception of the season) that gave the Dawgs a 26-21 victory. The next day, Georgia ascended to No. 1 in the polls, where it stayed through the end of the season, beating Notre Dame 17-10 in the Sugar Bowl to win the National Championship.

One little-known footnote: right tackle Nat Hudson's emergency reaction made the whole thing possible. On the play, Hudson peeled off his initial block to take on the defender breaking past the line of scrimmage and closing in on Belue. Without Hudson's quick-thinking pivot, Belue's pass never would have been thrown.

Here's Larry Munson's immortal call of that play:

"Florida in a stand-up five, they may or may not blitz, Belue third down on the 8, in trouble, he got a block behind him, going to throw on the run, complete on the 25 to the 30, Lindsay Scott 35, 40, Lindsay Scott 45, 50, 45, 40. . . . Run Lindsay! 25, 20, 15, 10, Lindsay Scott! Lindsay Scott! Lindsay Scott!"

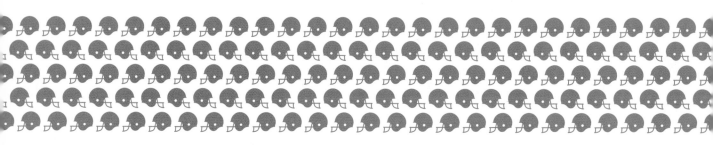

Georgia tailback Herschel Walker was a freshman that year. In his three cracks at Florida's defense before bolting for the New Jersey Generals of the USFL, Walker ran for 649 yards and eight touchdowns.

The rest of the '80s belonged to Georgia. In 1985, Florida sailed into Jacksonville ranked No. 1 in the nation to play the 6-1-1 Bulldogs. Energized by an 89-yard Tim Worley touchdown run, Georgia won 24-3 and torpedoed the Gators' title run.

The '90s were a different story. When Spurrier returned to his alma mater as coach in 1990, the ledger read 43-22-2, advantage Georgia. With Spurrier as coach, Florida won 11 of 12. In fact, entering the 2004 renewal, the Gators had taken 13 of the previous 14 from the Bulldogs.

But in 2004, Georgia scored on its opening drive with a 27-yard pass from David Greene to tight end Leonard Pope. A 35-yard Greene-to-Pope scoring strike followed later in the first period. The Bulldogs kept the pressure on, withstood a second half Gator rally and emerged with a 31-24 victory, and a 46-35-2 lead in the series.

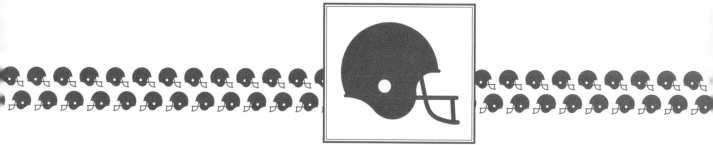

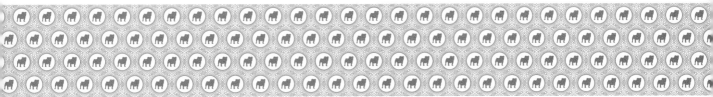

Georgia Tech

Georgia and Georgia Tech first met for football on Nov. 4, 1893 in a game won by Tech 28-6, though Georgia has long since taken the upper hand in the series. The intensity of the rivalry can best be described by the title of the book by author Bill Cromartie—*Clean Old-Fashioned Hate*—recounting its history. There was a five-year period (1920-24) when the two did not even play each other because of strained relations.

The 1942 contest matched the incredible talents of Georgia backs Frank Sinkwich and Charley Trippi. Tech entered the contest with a perfect 9-0 mark; the Bulldogs stood at 9-1. The SEC title was on the line and an invitation to the Rose Bowl was promised to the winner. Highlighted by an 85-yard touchdown run by Trippi, the Bulldogs rolled to a 34-0 win, the conference crown and Rose Bowl date with UCLA, which Georgia won 9-0.

Another renewal with the SEC title hanging in the balance came in 1948. Behind the splendid field generalship of quarterback Johnny Rauch, UGA took an 8-1 record into the game, including shutouts of LSU (22-0) and Alabama (35-0). The Dawgs led the Techsters 14-7 in the fourth quarter when Ken McCall scored on a 56-yard punt return to salt away the victory and bring to Athens a second conference championship in three years.

What is referred to by Georgia fans as "the Drought"—an eight-game losing streak in the Georgia Tech series—stretched from 1949 to 1956 as Tech coach Bobby Dodd held the upper hand over Georgia boss Wally Butts. The 1957 matchup, played in Atlanta, was scoreless in the third quarter when Theron Sapp took the game over, recovering a fumble at midfield from his linebacker position. Then playing fullback on offense, he practically willed the game's only touchdown, crashing for a first down at the 37, later in the drive picking up 25 yards on six straight carries into the Tech line and scoring from the 1 on fourth and goal. For almost single-handedly ending the drought, his number, 40, was retired upon his graduation following the 1958 season. He enjoyed a fine career and was All-SEC in 1958, but to Georgia fans he is lovingly remembered as "the Drought Breaker."

In 1966, Tech rolled into Sanford Stadium with a 9-0 record, highlighted by the sparkling backfield play of Kim King and Lenny Snow. Georgia, with Vince Dooley in his third year at the helm, was 8-1 and already had won the SEC title (Tech had withdrawn from the league two years earlier). Georgia's smothering defense, spearheaded by All-America tackle

George Patton, allowed King and Snow no room to maneuver. Kent Lawrence's 71-yard punt return ignited the Bulldogs' 23-14 victory that ruined Dodd's hopes for a perfect record in his final season as a head coach.

Georgia entered the 1971 contest at 9-1, having dropped from 9-0 against Auburn and quarterback Pat Sullivan. In a nationally televised Thanksgiving night game at Grant Field, the Bulldogs fell behind 14-0 early. Later in the game Georgia stormed back to 24-21 and took possession at its own 35 with less than a minute and a half remaining in the game. Quarterback Andy Johnson directed the winning touchdown drive, connecting on key passes to Mike Green and Bob Burns. His strike to Burns put the Bulldogs on the Tech 1 with 20 seconds to go. Running back Jimmy Poulos dove in from there for the 28-21 win.

The Dawgs took six in a row from Tech from 1978 to 1983, and seven in a row from 1991 to 1997. In the '97 contest, the Yellow Jackets took a 24-21 lead on a three-yard Charles Wiley run with 48 seconds left in the game. But the Dawgs came roaring back, driving 65 yards after the ensuing kickoff and scoring on an eight-yard Mike Bobo–to–Cory Allen pass to steal the 27-24 win in Atlanta.

Entering the 2005 campaign, Georgia enjoys a four-game winning streak in the Georgia Tech series. In 2004, with quarterback David Greene spending most of the game on the bench with a sprained thumb, the Bulldogs struggled offensively but still managed to escape with a 19-13 win and a healthy 56-36-5 lead in the series.

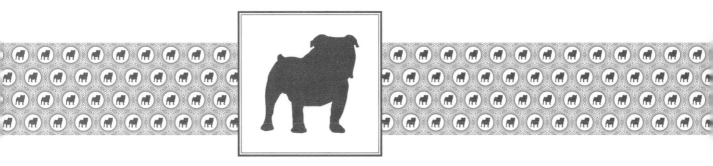

Auburn

Unlike some of the more bitter rivalries in college football, the Georgia-Auburn game has customarily been played amidst an atmosphere of sportsmanship. It has been described as a battle between brothers, and it is the Deep South's oldest rivalry.

Dr. Charles Herty, a chemistry professor at the University of Georgia, first introduced the game of football to the students. The first game ever played in the Deep South was a matchup between Georgia and Mercer, which had been arranged by Professor Herty, on Jan. 30, 1892. Immediately thereafter, Herty and an old Johns Hopkins classmate of his—Dr. George Petrie, a history professor at Auburn—set up a meeting between their two schools. The game was played in rain and mud on Feb. 20, 1892 at Atlanta's Piedmont Park. Auburn won 10-0 and a southern football institution was born. They met again in 1894, '95 and '96, with Georgia winning two of the three. Beginning in 1898, they have played every year except 1917 and '18 (World War I) and 1943 (World War II). Of their 108 meetings over the years, Auburn holds a slight 52-48-8 edge.

From 1916 through 1958, the game was played regularly at Columbus, Ga. Beginning in 1959, the series has been played on a home-and-home basis.

There's been no shortage of drama in this series. In 1933, the Southeastern Conference's inaugural season, Georgia was 7-0 and steaming toward the league championship when Auburn upended the Bulldogs' title run 14-6. One of the more dramatic finishes in the series came in 1941. The game was scoreless and Georgia had the ball at its own 36 with three seconds remaining. Frank Sinkwich took the snap, faded back and heaved the ball as far as he could, hoping speedster Lamar Davis would run under it. That's exactly what happened, and the Bulldogs escaped Columbus with a 7-0 win.

In 1942, Georgia was undefeated and headed toward a national title, with Sinkwich and the immortal Charley Trippi in the backfield. But with the Bulldogs looking ahead to the contest against coach William Alexander's second-ranked Georgia Tech team the following week, the Tigers snuck up and bit them, 27-13.

The Bulldogs needed a win over the Tigers to clinch the SEC title in 1959. The Tigers were also still alive for a share of the title, and jumped out to a 6-0 lead on a pair of field goals. But when Auburn punted out of its own end zone, Georgia's Charley Britt sprinted under the ball surrounded by the Auburn coverage unit and didn't stop until he had scored and put the Dogs on top 7-6. After a scoreless third quarter, Auburn retook the lead 13-7 in the fourth. That's when Bulldog quarterback Fran Tarkenton took over the game. With time running out, Tarkenton passed his team downfield with the precision of a surgeon. With 25 seconds left, Tarkenton rolled right, then stopped and

turned and found end Bill Herron with the game-winning touchdown pass. The drive had begun when a Georgia guard named Pat Dye recovered an Auburn fumble at the Tigers' 45.

It was a 248-yard, four-touchdown passing performance against sixth-ranked Georgia in 1971 that as much as anything else propelled fifth-ranked Auburn's quarterback, Pat Sullivan, to the Heisman Trophy that season. And it was 121-yard rushing game, including a 67–yard touchdown run against Georgia, that put Bo Jackson in the driver's seat for the Heisman in 1985.

But the Dawgs have used wins over Auburn to propel them to glory as well. Who can forget 1982, with Larry Munson exhorting the Bulldogs to "Hunker down one more time!" in a 19–14 win that clinched the SEC Championship.

In 1994, Auburn was riding a 20-game winning streak when the Bulldogs came calling at Jordan-Hare Stadium. Record-setting quarterback Eric Zeier led Georgia back from 23–9 down to a 23–23 tie, ruining the Tigers' drive for perfection. In 1996 at Auburn, the 100th game in the series, the Dogs and Tigers played the first overtime game in SEC history. Georgia trailed 28–14 in the fourth quarter before battling back to tie the score on the last play of regulation and win 56–49 in four overtimes.

In 2002 at Jordan-Hare, Georgia led Auburn for exactly 85 seconds. But it was the last 85 seconds. The Bulldogs trailed 21–17 when on fourth-and-15 quarterback David Greene lofted the ball to Michael Johnson, who leapt over an Auburn defender in the back left corner of the end zone and pulled the ball down with 1:25 left for the 24–21 win.

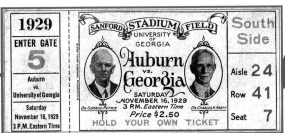

TALKIN' GEORGIA FOOTBALL

We thought we'd go straight to the source and let some of Georgia's greatest legends share their thoughts about Bulldog football.

*"**Even before the season, before the Tennessee game,** before he had touched the ball, there seemed to be a sense of anticipation. I wondered what great things Herschel had done in practice to cause it. Then he got the football and everyone knew. I've never seen anyone like him."*

GEORGIA'S FIRST HEISMAN WINNER, FRANK SINKWICH, ON ITS SECOND, HERSCHEL WALKER

"I can't understand why everyone is making such a fuss about me. I was never one to try and get my name in the papers. The credit should go to my teammates. They blocked. All I did was run."

HERSCHEL WALKER, DISCUSSING HIS RECORD-BREAKING HIGH SCHOOL CAREER

"There's nothing like a Saturday afternoon here in Athens,
and that's just something I had to find out about. I think I made the right decision. Now
I want to win the SEC after coming up short with Auburn the last two years. Tennessee is
going to start us off completely on the right foot or completely on the wrong foot."

BUCK BELUE, PRIOR TO THE 1980 SEASON

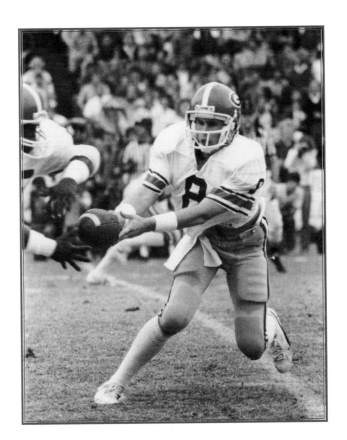

"I think of winning for Georgia first. I sincerely mean that. A lot of fellows say that and they think about All-SEC or All-American. The team must win for me to be satisfied. The only good thing about all these honors is that you can sit around and tell your kids about 'em one day on down the road." ALL-SEC LINEBACKER BEN ZAMBIASI, LEADER OF GEORGIA'S JUNKYARD DAWG DEFENSE IN THE MID-1970s

"A lot of pride goes with wearing those red hats. That is one of our rallying calls—'Stick the red hats to 'em.' When the going would get tough, you'd hear it from the sideline—'Stick 'em with the red hats.'" BILL STANFILL (ATHLON SOUTHEASTERN FOOTBALL, 1969)

"It isn't that we've had the very best players in the league. But we were united. There is a lot of spirit at Georgia. Almost everyone gets along with everyone else. The only real fight I remember was two B-teamers slugging it out to see who got into a scrimmage." BILL STANFILL IN ATHLON SPORTS

"My days at the University of Georgia were memorable for a number of reasons. Growing up in Athens and then playing for the Bulldogs was something I wanted to do, and then to play on a conference championship team enabled me to gain the confidence that I could play in the National Football League.

"When I first got to the NFL, I was confident I could win the starting job at quarterback because I had learned the passing game from the master. When Coach (Wallace) Butts drew pass patterns on the board, I was fascinated. He really knew what he was doing. No other team spent as much time on the passing game as we did. I don't know why coach Butts loved the passing game more than other coaches of his era, but he did.

"I played 18 years in the NFL, and the main reason that I was able to do that was the foundation I had when I entered the league. That foundation came from my quarterback experience under Coach Butts at Georgia."

GEORGIA ALL-AMERICAN AND COLLEGE AND NFL HALL OF FAMER FRAN TARKENTON

"I have to say there ain't a man alive who has more respect for Georgia than I do, and there will always be a place in my heart for Georgia. Georgia gave me the foundation that I would live the rest of my life on. And I can't really put into words how grateful I am for that." PAT DYE, AN ALL-AMERICA GUARD AT GEORGIA IN 1959-60 AND ONE OF FOUR DYE BROTHERS WHO PLAYED FOR GEORGIA. DYE WON FOUR SEC CHAMPIONSHIPS AS HEAD COACH AT AUBURN FROM 1981 TO 1992

"Of course, who can ever forget us kicking (Steve) Spurrier's butt the year he won the Heisman Trophy! It was one of those days where everything was clicking. If you go back and look at that film, you'll see that between George Patton and Bill Stanfill, Spurrier never had a chance to set up all day. It was total domination by those two guys." BILLY PAYNE, ALL-SEC DEFENSIVE END IN 1968 AND PRESIDENT AND CEO OF THE 1996 OLYMPIC GAMES IN ATLANTA

"*Despite all those wins the first three years,* I am most proud of our 1983 season, when I was captain. We lost Herschel (Walker), who turned pro early, and people were talking about what a disaster it was going to be. So we all got together and decided we were going to shock the world. We challenged everybody on that team to step up to the plate and take up the slack. And that's exactly what that team did.

"My group has a lot to be proud of. For now, when the Georgia fans are asked about the glory days, they always say 1980-1983. You gotta like that no matter how old you get. All I know is that it's been 20 years since I played, and I can still walk into a crowded room and somebody will say, 'Hey, there's Freddie Gilbert. He played football for Georgia.' That's still pretty neat." FREDDIE GILBERT, ALL-AMERICA DEFENSIVE END IN 1983 AND TWO-TIME ALL-SEC PERFORMER. GILBERT WAS CAPTAIN OF THE 1983 TEAM THAT FINISHED 10-1-1.

"My job was to go down and do a little curl pattern. I didn't know what was going on behind the line of scrimmage. All I knew was that Buck got me the ball, and when I caught it I knew I had the first down.

"But at that moment, my mind went back to something that John Donaldson had taught me in high school. He always said, 'Don't fall; keep on running after you catch the ball.' So when I caught the ball and felt myself going down, I put my hand on the ground to steady myself and kept running. Once I got my balance, I saw a guy go down, and then I saw an opening.

"When I started running my first thought was that I could get us into field goal range. After about 10 more yards it dawned on me, 'Hell, I can take this thing to the house.'"
LINDSAY SCOTT, ON THE PLAY

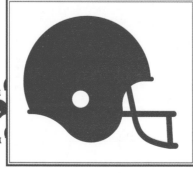

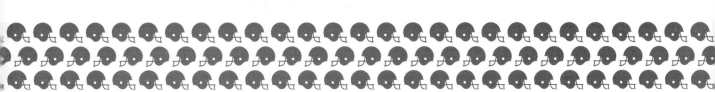

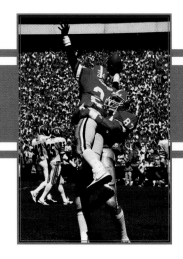

FACTS AND FIGURES

Bowl Game Scores

RECORD: 22-15-3			
DATE	**BOWL**	**OPPONENT**	**SCORE**
Jan. 1, 1942	Orange	TCU	40-26
Jan. 1, 1943	Rose	UCLA	9-0
Jan. 1, 1946	Oil	Tulsa	20-6
Jan. 1, 1947	Sugar	North Carolina	20-10
Jan. 1, 1948	Gator	Maryland	20-20
Jan. 1, 1949	Orange	Texas	28-41
Dec. 9, 1950	Presidential Cup	Texas A&M	20-40
Jan. 1, 1960	Orange	Missouri	14-0
Dec. 26, 1964	Sun	Texas Tech	7-0
Dec. 31, 1966	Cotton	SMU	24-9
Dec. 16, 1967	Liberty	NC State	7-14
Jan. 1, 1969	Sugar	Arkansas	2-16
Dec. 20, 1969	Sun	Nebraska	6-45
Dec. 31, 1971	Gator	North Carolina	7-3

DATE	BOWL	OPPONENT	SCORE
Dec. 28, 1973	Peach	Maryland	17-16
Dec. 21, 1974	Tangerine	Miami (Ohio)	10-21
Jan. 1, 1976	Cotton	Arkansas	10-31
Jan. 1, 1977	Sugar	Pittsburgh	3-27
Dec. 31, 1978	Bluebonnet	Stanford	22-25
Jan. 1, 1981	Sugar	Notre Dame	17-10
Jan. 1, 1982	Sugar	Pittsburgh	20-24
Jan. 1, 1983	Sugar	Penn State	23-27
Jan. 2, 1984	Cotton	Texas	10-9
Dec. 22, 1984	Citrus	Florida State	17-17
Dec. 28, 1985	Sun	Arizona	13-13
Dec. 23, 1986	Hall of Fame	Boston College	24-27
Dec. 29, 1987	Liberty	Arkansas	20-17
Jan. 1, 1989	Gator	Michigan State	34-27
Dec. 30, 1989	Peach	Syracuse	18-19
Dec. 29, 1991	Independence	Arkansas	24-15
Jan. 1, 1993	Florida Citrus	Ohio State	21-14
Dec. 30, 1995	Peach	Virginia	27-34
Jan. 1, 1998	Outback	Wisconsin	33-6
Dec. 31, 1998	Peach	Virginia	35-33
Jan. 1, 2000	Outback	Purdue	28-25
Dec. 24, 2000	O'ahu	Virginia	37-14
Dec. 28, 2001	Music City	Boston College	16-20
Jan. 1, 2003	Sugar	Florida State	26-13
Jan. 1, 2004	Capital One	Purdue	34-27
Jan. 1, 2005	Outback	Wisconsin	24-21

Career Statistical Leaders

Rushes: 994, Herschel Walker, 1980-82

Rushing Yards: 5,259, Herschel Walker, 1980-82

Rushing Touchdowns: 49, Herschel Walker, 1980-82

Pass Attempts: 1,440, David Greene, 2001-04

Pass Completions: 849, David Greene, 2001-04

Passing Yards: 11,528, David Greene, 2001-04

Touchdown Passes: 72, David Greene, 2001-04

Total Offense Yards: 11,274, David Greene, 2001-04

Pass Receptions: 204, Terrence Edwards, 1999-2002

Receiving Yards: 3,093, Terrence Edwards, 1999-2002

Touchdown Catches: 30, Terrence Edwards, 1999-2002

Points Scored: 409, Billy Bennett, 2000-03

Kickoff Return Average (Min. 20): 25.5 yards, Andre Hastings, 1990-92

Punt Return Average (Min. 25): 14.2 yards, Zippy Morocco, 1949-51

Total Tackles: 467, Ben Zambiasi, 1974-77

Sacks: 36, David Pollack, 2001-04

Interceptions: 16, Jake Scott, 1967-68

Bulldogs in the Pros

Boss Bailey, LB, Detroit Lions

Champ Bailey, CB, Denver Broncos

Kendrell Bell, LB, Kansas City Chiefs

Terreal Bierria, DB, Seattle Seahawks

Reggie Brown, WR, Philadelphia Eagles

Chris Clemons, LB, Washington Redskins

Nic Clemons, DE, Washington Redskins

Antonio Cochran, DE, Seattle Seahawks

Kentrell Curry, DB, Detroit Lions

Phillip Daniels, DE, Washington Redskins

Thomas Davis, LB, Carolina Panthers

Demetric Evans, DE, Washington Redskins

Jason Ferguson, DT, Dallas Cowboys

George Foster, OL, Denver Broncos

Robert Geathers, DE, Cincinnati Bengals

Fred Gibson, WR, Pittsburgh Steelers

Tony Gilbert, LB, Jacksonville Jaguars

Randall Godfrey, LB, San Diego Chargers

Charles Grant, DE, New Orleans Saints

David Greene, QB, Seattle Seahawks

Arnold Harrison, LB, Pittsburgh Steelers

Verron Haynes, RB, Pittsburgh Steelers

Steve Herndon, OG, Atlanta Falcons

Jonas Jennings, OL, San Francisco 49ers

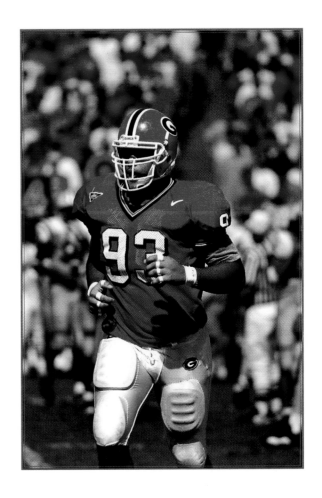

Sean Jones, SS, Cleveland Browns

John Kasay, PK, Carolina Panthers

Randy McMichael, TE, Miami Dolphins

Patrick Pass, RB, New England Patriots

Todd Peterson, PK, Atlanta Falcons

Jermaine Phillips, DB, Tampa Bay Bucs

David Pollack, LB, Cincinnati Bengals

Richard Seymour, DT, New England Patriots

Musa Smith, RB, Baltimore Ravens

Jon Stinchcomb, OL, New Orleans Saints

Matt Stinchcomb, OT, Tampa Bay Bucs

Mack Strong, FB, Seattle Seahawks

Marcus Stroud, DT, Jacksonville Jaguars

Johnathan Sullivan, DT, New Orleans Saints

Jeremy Thomas, FB, Cincinnati Bengals

Bruce Thornton, CB, Dallas Cowboys

Odell Thurman, LB, Cincinnati Bengals

J.T. Wall, FB, Indianapolis Colts

Hines Ward, WR, Pittsburgh Steelers

Ben Watson, TE, New England Patriots

Jermaine Wiggins, TE, Minnesota Vikings

Will Witherspoon, LB, Carolina Panthers

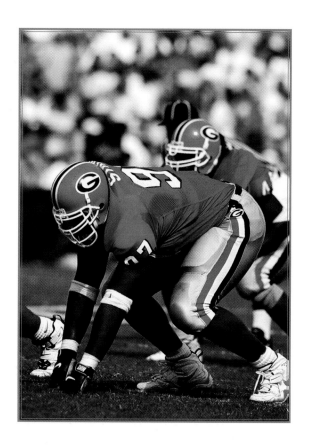

First-Round Draft Picks

E Harry Babcock, 1952, Pittsburgh Steelers; 1953, San Francisco 49ers

CB Champ Bailey, 1999, Washington Redskins

DB Thomas Davis, 2005, Carolina Panthers

RB Robert Edwards, 1998, New England Patriots

OL George Foster, 2003, Denver Broncos

DE Charles Grant, 2002 New Orleans Saints

RB Rodney Hampton, 1990, New York Giants

RB Garrison Hearst, 1993, Arizona Cardinals

LB David Pollack, 2005, Cincinnati Bengals

WR Lindsay Scott, 1982, New Orleans Saints

DT Richard Seymour, 2001, New England Patriots

RB Frank Sinkwich, 1943, Detroit Lions

DB Ben Smith, 1990, Philadelphia Eagles

OG Royce Smith, 1972, New Orleans Saints

DE Bill Stanfill, 1969, Miami Dolphins

OT Matt Stinchcomb, 1999, Oakland Raiders

DT Marcus Stroud, 2001 Jacksonvile Jaguars

DT Jonathan Sullivan, 2003, New Orleans Saints

HB Charley Trippi, 1947, St. Louis Cardinals

OT Bernard Williams, 1994, Philadelphia Eagles

RB Tim Worley, 1989, Pittsburgh Steelers

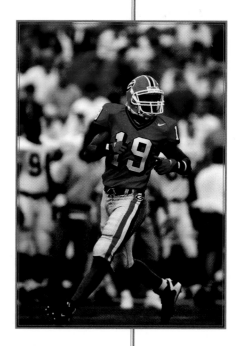

FROM THE ARCHIVES

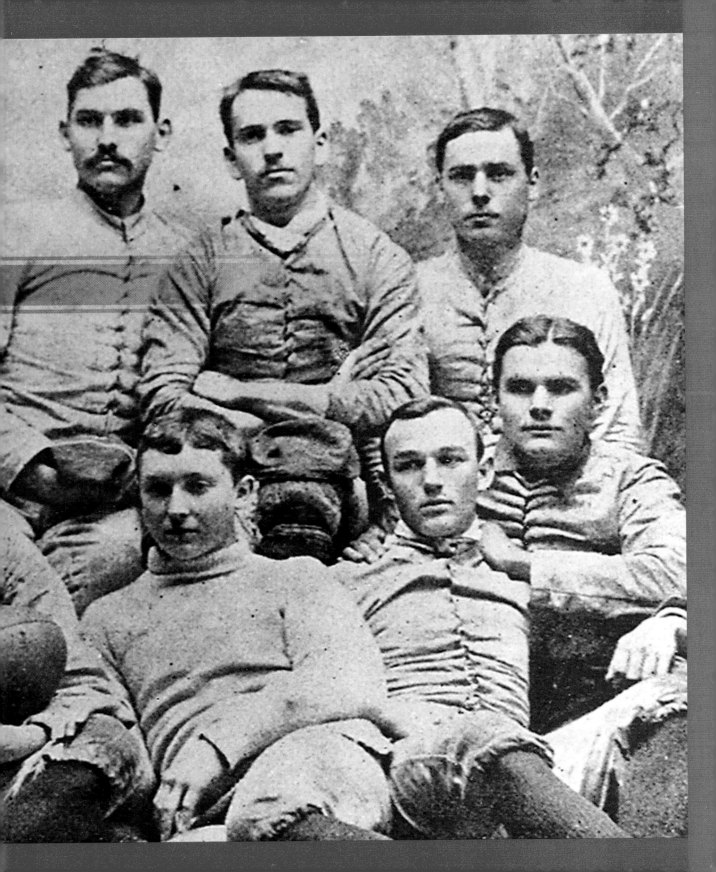

The 1966 Georgia Bulldogs

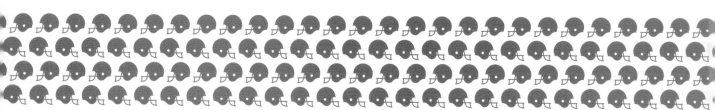

143

The 1976 Georgia Bulldogs

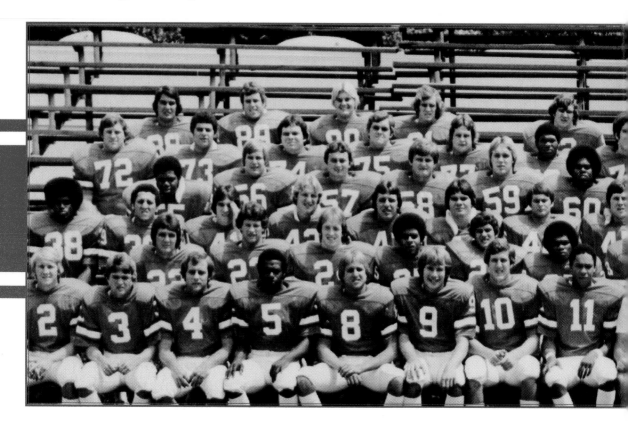

The 1980 Georgia Bulldogs